Living Intentionally:
A Six-step Transformation from Goal-Setting to Goal-Getting

Workbook

By: Dr. Bonnie Aaron

Living Intentionally Workbook: A Six-step Transformation from Goal-setting to Goal-getting

livingintentionally@keenshipllc.com

ISBN 10: 0990341720

ISBN 13: 978-0-9903417-2-7

Book interior design by Abigail Michel https://www.elance.com/s/amicheleditor

Cover Design by Kiran https://www.elance.com/s/anjum-liaqat/

"Thoughts determine what you want. Action determines what you get."

Author Unknown

CONTENTS

Be the change that you want to see in the world.

Mahatma Gandhi

INTRODUCTION

You can get much of what you want in life but first, you have to know what you want and give yourself permission to want it. When you are ready to transform your life, you will search for answers to life's questions and there you will find that the truest answers come from within. This workbook provides plenty of writing space because the most important part of the book will be the thoughts, ideas and answers that you write. When you accept the fact that you possess the answers inside yourself and take responsibility for the pattern of life you can create, you will be happier and more successful.

As you put your thoughts on paper, you will discover the personal power you have always possessed. The engagement activities in this workbook will provide strategies for those who may struggle with negative thought patterns. Whether you struggle with negative patterns such as anger, doubt, fear, self-limiting beliefs or insecurity, this workbook will be helpful to you. Each chapter will lead you on a journey into yourself, confront the important questions, and challenge your excuses.

You can choose from many paths as you travel on the road to personal success. If you do not know your destination, you will not know which path to take. As you observe people, you will notice the masses of people drifting aimlessly until they come to a fork in the road; as did Alice when she asked the Cheshire Cat for directions:

"Which road shall I take?"
"That depends on where you want to go."
"I don't know where I want to go."
"Well then, any road will do."

The cat was correct in his advice, but if you actually want to get somewhere, any road will not do. At least Alice was conscious enough to realize a decision had to be made when she reached the crossroads. Even if you are not sure which route to take, your beliefs and values should determine the destination, making the decision clear when approaching crossroads. This workbook will help you determine your destination and draw your own map.

This workbook has made it into your hands because you are ready to transform your life. Buddha teaches, "When the student is ready, the teacher appears." The process of redirecting your life is often painful, slow, and sometimes complex.

Pick a day to start anew. Webster defines new as "refreshed, different from one of the same that has existed previously; unfamiliar." Yes, sometimes the reasons for the changes in your life are scary because they are unfamiliar. However, changing directions and beginning a new phase of your life's journey is refreshing and invigorating. Wherever you are, start there.

One of the goals for writing the book is to help you explore the possibilities and choices awaiting you. Each of the six steps in the workbook poses questions only you can answer. Every year, on your birthday, get a copy of this workbook and complete the guided practice exercises. As you document your progress each year, you will be able to see how much you have grown. Each year you will learn something new about yourself because you will be a different person. The explanation and rationale behind each of the practice activities is contained in the accompanying book *Living Intentionally: A Six-step Transformation (2014)*. Self-evaluation and self-reflection will result in self-discovery.

The steps you are about to implement can change your life. You will learn how to unlock the great untapped reserves of potential that lie deep within you. The steps outlined are intensely practical. Each step contains exercises for you. They are designed to empower you with the tools you need to take complete control of your life, and for these tools to work, you must practice with them. You must discipline yourself to do the exercises in sequence so you receive the full benefit of their cumulative effect.

The material that follows is a six-step guide to direct you to take action toward your personal transformation. Each step reveals a timeless truth, offers practical application tips, and issues a call to action. There is no question that while we retain very little of what we read, we retain nearly all of what we do. In the guided practice steps that follow, you will do far more than you will read. You will benefit most from practice.

You will be surprised to find the answers you seek to life's questions are found in your own mind through studying, searching, and pondering and revealed in the form of a plan, idea, or inspiration. Your answers are the stepping stones that connect the bridge from goal-setting to goal-getting.

STEP ONE: DISCOVER YOUR PURPOSE

WHAT IS YOUR PURPOSE?

The bridge between what you want to do and taking action is having a definite purpose. Your purpose statement should connect with the passion that provides a compelling reason to live a higher life. You can make a difference in the decisions you make, goals you set, and your achievements when you apply your purpose statement to everything you do.

Throughout this workbook ask yourself the following three questions so your answers will be aligned with your purpose statement.

1. What is the purpose?
2. What should I be doing?
3. What is really worth doing?

The next two exercises will help you prepare for writing a purpose statement.

The first exercise is to make a list of what you want to accomplish in your life (personally, spiritually, and professionally):

WHAT I WANT TO ACCOMPLISH

Personally	Spiritually	Professionally

You may know exactly what you want to do, but you may not know how to go about getting started. Take knowing what you want to do with your life to the next level of doing. Take all your dreams, wants, and desires and add the missing ingredient-action.

Living your purpose statement will leave a lasting legacy for your posterity. The process of creating a purpose statement will lead to discovery and learning how to fulfill your purpose. One of the greatest benefits of living purposefully is the freedom to express your deepest beliefs about what gives meaning and value to your life.

The second exercise includes answering some empowering questions designed to help you think at a higher level:

What point in my life did I feel invincible, full of energy, focused, and determined?

What was I doing to make me feel driven?

If I only had one year left to live, what would be the greatest gift I would give?

If I was guaranteed that anything I did would be successful, what would I do?

Practice asking these questions to friends and family. At first the questions may not be received very well. The questions make people very uncomfortable. If the response is "I do not know," then follow up with, "Well, if you DID know, then what would the answer be?" That question does not go over well. Wait a few weeks and pose the same questions to the same people. With a little brainstorming, most people are able to come up with something just to get you to go away.

Notes: (What were your thoughts as you answered the four questions on page 4?)
(What kind of responses did you receive when you practiced asking those four questions to family and friends?)

THE FOLLOWING PRACTICE ACTIVITIES WILL HELP YOU DEVELOP A WRITTEN PURPOSE STATEMENT

Part 1

Inspiration—Think of a quote, or verse from a song or poem that inspires you. Think of a phrase or saying you use to get you through a situation. Use this guiding phrase as an anchor.

Examples: with God all things are possible; what does not kill you makes you stronger; pay it forward, celebrate the good days.

My anchor phrase:

Notes

_____

_____

_____

_____

_____

_____

_____

Part 2

Roles—Think of all the different roles you play in life, where and how you spend most of your time, and what interests occupy your thoughts.

Examples: parent, spouse, friend, employee, author, teacher, student, manager

Roles I play:

-
-
-
-

            -
            -
            -
            -

Notes: (What interests occupy your thoughts?)

Part 3

Interests—Write down interests that are common throughout all major areas of your life.

Examples: *serving others, teaching, photography, learning*

I am interested in:

-
-
-
-

-
-
-
-

From the list of interests, sort out the gifts and talents with which you have been blessed. These are the strengths you will need to fulfill your purpose. These gifts will help you sustain and maintain your pursuit of purpose-driven living.

CATEGORIES OF INTERESTS

GIFTS	TALENTS	HOBBIES
Example: serving others	*teaching*	*photography*

Part 4

Role Models and Mentors—Name role models and mentors with whom you look up to and admire. Role models and mentors will help you discover the truths of life that have already stood the test of time.

With whom do I spend the most time? (You are the average of the five people with which you spend the most time.)
Example: coworkers, family, friends

_____   _____

_____   _____

_____   _____

_____   _____

_____   _____

Who do I look up to and admire?
Example: religious leaders, thought leaders, relatives, business icons

_____   _____

_____   _____

_____   _____

_____   _____

What qualities do they possess that I admire most?
Example: work ethics, integrity, grit, humility

_____

_____

_____

_____

_____

Some of your strongest character traits may be the same or similar to your gifts listed in Part 3 or qualities of others listed in this part. The characteristics on the following list must be those you already possess; they need to be identified as useful tools to achieving a purposeful life.

My strongest character traits are:
Example: optimistic, intelligent, honest

_____

_____

_____

_____

_____

Part 5

Outcomes—What do I really want to accomplish? What are my expectations? What actions must I take to be successful?

Example: The fruits of my labors will be cultivated in service to others.

I really want to accomplish_____.

My expectations are _____.

I must take the following actions to accomplish success _____

_____.

Write an outcome statement using the information you provided above.

_____

_____

Notes

_____

_____

_____

_____

CREATE YOUR PURPOSE STATEMENT

Now that you have practiced thinking intentionally, the following guided activity will help you develop your purpose statement. Your purpose statement is the answer to the question, "What is my purpose in life?" Now that you have established an anchor, identified strengths you possess and those you admire, you are ready to create your purpose statement. Some people write separate purpose statements for their personal, professional, and spiritual life. In the following activity you will focus on the purpose of your life as a whole.

Make a three part outline to give your statement clarity:
>   1st -Guiding anchor
>   2nd -List some strengths that will help you achieve your purpose
>   3rd -What action will you take and why

Example: The purpose of my life is to celebrate life (anchor) with a positive attitude (strength) so I can edify and uplift others (action and why).

If you draw a blank, begin writing your mission statement with "I believe . . . . " or "The purpose of my life is . . ." Write a rough draft and ask a few friends or family members to review and offer feedback. Ask what they liked best and if it is true to who you are. Make any necessary revisions for the final copy. Post the purpose statement in a place you will read it regularly. The best recommendation is to memorize it and you can recite it to serve as a constant reminder to live life purposefully.

MY PURPOSE STATEMENT OUTLINE:

1st -Guiding anchor:

2nd -Strengths that will help me achieve my purpose:

3rd -Action I will take and why:

MY PURPOSE STATEMENT:

ARE YOU READY FOR A TRANSFORMATION?

Step One of this workbook is the starting point to finding out if you are ready and willing to begin your transformation. The questions below will help you determine your readiness.

With your purpose statement in mind, answer the following questions.

What do I desire more than anything?

If I received what I asked for, what would I receive?

Am I ready for it right now?

If I had complete certainly I would succeed, what actions would I take to pursue my dreams?

What obstacles prevent me from achieving my dreams right now?

What am I willing to do to get what I really want?

After you have finished all of the activities in this workbook you will answer those same questions again. Hopefully, your answers will be more insightful as a result of defining your life's purpose. You may even find that the purpose statement you wrote initially needs revising.

In your quest for discovering your purpose, you will not only be asked to answer many questions but you will practice asking the right questions. There is an art to asking the right questions as you search for your purpose.

Notes
_____

_____

_____

_____

_____

_____

_____

_____

_____

_____

_____

FINDING PURPOSE IN YOUR ADVERSITY

When faced with difficult situations many people begin asking all the wrong questions. For instance, when faced with adversity the majority of people ask disempowering questions such as, "Why me?" or "What is wrong with me?"

What wrong questions do you ask when faced with a difficult situation?

Example: Why wasn't I born into a rich family?

Stop asking the wrong questions because they lead to nowhere. **Instead practice asking a better question.**

Example: What steps can I take to increase my income?

Consistently asking the same question is a sign you are not ready to take decisive action. **Think of a question you consistently ask.**

Example: I continue to ask, "Why can't I win the lottery?"

I continue to ask:

Maybe you continue to ask the same question because you do not like the answer, or are you avoiding the answer because you are not ready to proceed. If persistent questioning does not result in answers, the answer is probably no. If the answers received are not satisfying, then perhaps the wrong question has been posed. **Asking the right questions takes practice so practice framing better questions.**

Example: The question I should be asking is, "What steps can I take to achieve success?"

The questions I should be asking are:

Notes

STEP TWO: WHAT IS NOT WORKING

MAKING EXCUSES FOR FAILURE IS NOT WORKING

One trait unsuccessful people have in common is they have plenty of excuses for failure. Excuses prevent you from fulfilling your purpose. Some excuses include the following:

- *If only I had a good education*
- *If only I had a better job*
- *If only I made more money*
- *If only I were younger*
- *If only I had more time*

List some of your "if only" excuses for not fulfilling your purpose:

If only I _____

If only I_____

If only I_____

Creating excuses is not only a common trait among low achievers, it is a deeply rooted habit. People strongly defend their excuses because they created them. Defense mechanisms are excuses used to avoid living intentionally. Excuses for not living intentionally must be identified before they can be addressed and eliminated. Here are some more common excuses for not fulfilling your purpose:

- *Both of my parents are obese; therefore, I am genetically predisposed to being overweight.*
- *I cannot afford to go to college; therefore, I will continue to work for low wages.*

List specific excuses you defend:

Now that you have recognized some of the barriers you allow to prevent your progress, you can use them to complete the following exercises.

Notes

_____

_____

_____

_____

_____

_____

WORRY

Worries are the same as negative thoughts. A famous American psychologist says, "Worry is a spasm of the emotion; the mind catches hold of something and will not let it go." Consider the following questions as you complete the following activities.

- What worries paralyze you with fear and keep you from living intentionally?
- What problems stand in the way of performing at your full potential?
- Who are the people in your life who bring you down?

You may find many reasons to justify worrying. More importantly, you may find many more solutions to combat unhealthy worrying. One effective approach is to postpone worrying to a designated "worry period" of approximately 20 minutes. During the course of the day (or night) write your worries down on paper and save them for the worry period. Go over the list of worries only during the designated worry period. Outside of the 20 minute worry period, the rest of your day is worry-free. If the list of worries is short or no longer significant, end the worry period and enjoy the rest of the day. As you discipline your mind to postpone anxious thoughts, you will gain more confidence in your ability to control worrying. Try scheduling your list of worries on your phone for a specific time each day. As worries enter your mind throughout the day, add them to your list of scheduled worries.

MY WORRY PERIOD: _____
Example: 7:00-7:30 P.M.

MY LIST OF WORRIES
Example: No one will like my book.

1._____

2._____

3._____

For the next exercise, use the worries from the list on page 21 and enter them below. Then write a replacement thought that will cancel the worry.

WORRY	REPLACEMENT
Example: No one will like my book.	*Someone will love my book.*

Excessive worrying does not work for you. Cognitive therapy will work for you.

Notes

_____

_____

_____

_____

_____

_____

NEGATIVE THOUGHTS

The following exercise will help you stop a negative thought and replace it with a positive one.

Negative Thought Replacement Exercise

Think of two reoccurring negative thoughts (not on your worry list) and practice making substitutions.

Example: I doubt I have what it takes to start a business.

1.

2.

Replace the negative thoughts.

Negative Thought	REPLACEMENT
Example: I doubt I have what it takes to start a business.	*I will take inventory of all my skills and experiences that are necessary to start a successful business*

The next exercise will help you identify strong emotions that cause behaviors that are not working in your personal development.

Identify strong emotions you already know are triggers to undesirable behaviors.

1. Think about the root cause of jealousy that makes your heart race and your blood pressure rise. Just thinking about being jealous can change your physiology. You have just proven to yourself you have control over your emotions because you created an emotion just by thinking about situations that cause you to be jealous.

   Cause of jealousy:

2. Think of a time when you felt the rage of jealousy. **Ask yourself the following questions**:

   • **How did I act on that passion?**

   • **Did I yell at someone?**

   • **Did I throw something?**

   • **How did I vent all the emotions that built up?**

3. **Reflect on what thinking positive and healthy feelings will create.**

4. **Think about people you love and the emotions that make you feel good inside.** Reminisce about a time you felt overwhelmed with love for someone that you could not help but give them a big hug. You consciously lowered your blood pressure by going to a happy place.

NOTE: Whether you felt compelled to show the rage of jealousy or love and affection, you demonstrated emotion followed by action.

Exercise Notes:

STOP DOING WHAT DOES NOT WORK

Identify fears that paralyze you and hinder your personal progress. **List your top ten fears.**

MY TOP TEN FEARS
Example: Failure

1.

2.

3.

4.

5.

6

7.

8.

9.

10.

Jot down a few notes and think about the following questions about your fears while you work on the Negative Thoughts Exercise.

What are the root causes of my fears?

Which fears cause constant worry?

Which fears cause anxiety?

Notes

_____

_____

_____

_____

_____

_____

_____

_____

_____

Fill in the following table with the negative thoughts associated with the ten fears you listed on page 26.

NEGATIVE THOUGHTS CAUSED BY FEARS

FEAR	Negative Thought (doubt, self-limiting beliefs, anxiety and worry)
Example: failure	*I doubt I have what it take to start a business.*

YOUR IDENTITY

Self-imposed identities deny people opportunities to suffer well. **List some of the ways you allow adversity to define your identity:**
Example: Mom with the addicted daughter, Son with the alcoholic father

-

-

-

-

-

-

Everyone will eventually have the opportunity to experience pain and suffering. The outcome lies in the answer to the following questions:

- **Will you suffer poorly or well?**

- **Where does your gauge point on the adversity continuum?**

- **Will adversity stop you in your tracks or will it be the fuel that drives you to higher elevations?**

THE ARRIVAL FALLACY

Along the journey of life you must focus on the destination. Do not suspend happiness as a reward waiting for you when you reach your goals. Why postpone happiness until the end of the journey?   The following examples depict the anxious anticipation of the end of your journey:

Examples:

I will be happy when <u>I land my dream job</u>.

I will be happy when <u>I lose 20 pounds</u>.

I will be happy when <u>the kids are all raised</u>.

I will be happy when <u>I retire.</u>

I will be happy when <u>I win the lottery</u>.

Now it is your turn to practice:

I will be happy when _____.

I will be happy when _____.

I will be happy when _____.

I will be happy when _____.

I will be happy when _____.

Suspending happiness until your goals are accomplished is only a dream that continues to outdistance you. The actual journey itself is the true joy of the experience called life.

PAIN VS PLEASURE

The following are some examples of prolonging pleasure and happiness to avoid pain and suffering:

- *Asking my boss for a raise seems more painful than not asking. I am suspending the pleasure of possibly increasing my income.*
- *Committing to a healthy diet is more painful than eating unhealthy foods. I am suspending the pleasure of eating nutritiously and being healthy.*
- *Continuing an education is more painful than avoiding going back to school. I am suspending the pleasure of upgrading my skills for a career.*

For the following activity fill in the blank to fit what currently causes you pain:

Example: I will change when the pain to <u>exercise</u> is less than the pain to <u>remain overweight</u>.

I will change when the pain to _____

    is less than the pain to _____.

I will change when the pain to _____

    is less than the pain to _____.

Successful people agree that success is the ability to direct pain and pleasure instead of allowing pain and pleasure to direct them. That is the secret to gaining control of your life instead of life controlling you. There may be times in your life when circumstances out of your control will initiate a transformation.

DISEMPOWERING RULES DO NOT WORK

You may have a rule that the only way you feel loved is if everyone accepts your views. Not only is this rule unrealistic, you would not win the game very often because you have no control over the players. The players involved in your life probably do not know the rules. You should not be upset with those who break your rules. Keep in mind the rules are what cause the upset not the behavior of others. If you do not clearly communicate what the rules are, you cannot expect others to abide by them.

Contemplate the following thought-provoking questions:

What is an example of one of your life's rules that results in pain?

Example: The house must be cleaned to my satisfaction.

What rules determine what has to happen in order for you to feel successful?

Example: I must earn six figures before I feel successful.

Rule 1:_____

Rule 2:_____

What rules of life have you established that make life's game insurmountable for you?

Example: I feel everyone must like me; that makes life's game unsurmountable.

Rule 1:_____

Rule 2:_____

Rules of your game depend on the actions of others and some rules only involve yourself. Evaluate your rules and determine which rules depend on the actions of others to determine if the game is successful. Concentrate on the rules of your life's game that depend only on your actions to determine if the game is successful.

Notes

ASKING THE RIGHT QUESTIONS

The solution to your problems lie in the questions you ask. Reflective questioning causes you to refocus your attention on deciding what the correct question is before you can seek the right answer. The way you act or react to adversity may be what is not working. These are the right questions to ask.

When faced with adversity ask yourself the following questions:

What do I want life to look like on the other side of my adversity?

If there was a guarantee I could not fail, what would I do?

What one great wish would I dare to dream if I knew I could not fail?

Contemplate what can be done to achieve your dreams as quickly as possible.

Notes

STEP THREE: ELEVATE YOUR CONSCIOUSNESS

ACCOMPLISHMENTS/YOUR SUCCESS

The following activities are designed to raise or elevate your consciousness as you embark on your transformation. You have already experienced many successes in your life.

List some of your accomplishments.

<u>**My accomplishments:**</u>

Example: two beautiful children, Bachelor's Degree, lost 30 pounds

Now think of the common denominator that was your energy source of motivation.

What are the secrets to your success?

Example: persistence, grit, planning, organization

As you experience success you also experience failures. As you raise your awareness about your sources of effective motivation think about the motivational strategies that do not work for you.

Motivation

The first step in designing a customized motivational strategy is identifying what has not worked in the past. Identify the strategies you will STOP implementing because they have not proven to be effective.

Identify one motivational strategy that is not working for you:

_____ is not working for me because

_____.

The next time someone seeks your advice about a problem he/she is having, write down the advice you offer him/her. What do your answers reveal about yourself? Are they possibly the same answers to your own questions? The secret to what motivates you lies in your answers. Is your advice something you need or would like to receive? You may not always understand what others need or expect from you, but you can take your own advice. The advice you offer to others comes from within, so find a way to take your own advice.

Recently someone asked for my advice about _____,

and the solution I offered was _____.

The following steps will help you identify your personal motivational tools. One step to find out what motivates you is to ask a trusted friend what motivational strategies they think will work for you. Write down all of the answers because then you will have an arsenal of motivational tools to employ in your battle for success.

Motivational strategies my friends suggest work for me:

Friend #1_____

Friend #2 _____

A variety of motivational strategies exist, and your job is to implement the style that works best for you.

My motivational strategies:

1. _____

2. _____

3. _____

Using the right tools will equip you to achieve your dreams. Go out there and get the right motivational tools, and you will show yourself how winners really win.

AFFIRMATIONS

Affirmations are replacements for self-limiting negative thoughts (beliefs). Affirmations are a declaration of truth-a positive statement.

Covey identifies the following five basic ingredients to a positive affirmation:

1. Personal
2. Positive
3. Present tense
4. Visual
5. Filled with emotion

An example of a positive affirmation is:

I am extremely excited (emotional) when I (personal) achieve (present tense) my goal to lose five pounds (positive).

Positive affirmations that include the basic ingredients override negative information (beliefs) and reinforce new, positive thoughts which lead to new behavior.

See Practice Below.

Practice

I feel _____(emotion)

       when I (personal) _____(present tense)

            my _____(positive).

The following is an example of an affirmation with a supportive "because" statement that creates momentum toward your outcomes.

Example: I know <u>I can start my own business</u> because <u>people are interested in my photography</u>.

I know _____

because _____.

Today I begin a new life. Practice writing and saying aloud positive affirmations. Write statements in the first-person singular (present tense) as if it is already true.

Example: I have all the money and resources I need to make a contribution to this world.

I…

I…

You were born with instinctive ways to motivate and activate in order to survive and thrive. Step Four will guide you through the steps to being your own change agent.

WHAT IS YOUR FOCUS?

What gets your attention gets you. The law of attraction manifests negative statements just the same as positive affirmations. Identify a negative statement that has materialized because you invested so much attention in it. Reflect on your thoughts, worries, and prayers. Many of those conversations are expressed in the negative. For instance, if I pray that I will not flunk my test then I am focusing on flunking my test. My brain picks up on the emotions conjured up when contemplating flunking my test. Instead I should pray that I will be able to remember all that I have studied.

What do I consistently wish will NOT happen?

Turn the statement into a positive affirmation:

Discipline yourself to think and act on what you do want and off of what you do not want. Examples of effective questions include the following:

What do I really want to do with my life?

What outcomes make me the happiest?

1. _____

2. _____

3. _____

Fill out the following table identifying what you do not want to happen and how you can make it into a positive statement.

What I do NOT want to happen	What I DO want to happen
Example: I pray I will NOT get sick.	*Example: I pray I will be healthy.*

WHAT ARE YOUR DREAMS?

Take inventory of your dreams, beliefs, wishes, and desires

Write specific details to create your visualization inventory using the prompts below:

I dream of _____

I believe _____

I wish _____

I desire _____

I will share my inventory with _____

Write down all the dreams you wish will come true:
Example: I dream of <u>opening my own business</u>.

I dream of _____

I dream of _____

I dream of _____

I dream of _____

1. Imagine a possible future event that you dream about often.

2. Write a description of what this imaginary event will look like when it takes place.

3. What would it take to make it happen?

4. What does the end result look like?

5. Map your dream backwards beginning with the desired destination to the starting place where you are today. Begin mapping your dream on the next page.

Destination:_____

Step 5_____

Step 4_____

Step 3_____

Step 2_____

Step 1_____

Where I am today:_____

BE AWARE OF YOUR HABITS

My list of all the mindless, useless, or unimportant habits that I will STOP doing:

Example: Checking Facebook

1. _____

2. _____

3. _____

4. _____

5. _____

In order to strengthen the driving forces in your life, you must stop the restraining forces that impede progression. This can be accomplished if you have self-efficacy—you believe what you can achieve. Now that you have freed up some of your valuable time by eliminating useless habits, you can replace those habits with productive tasks.

Substitute each useless task listed previously with a productive task:

Example: Write 5 things for which I am grateful.

1. _____

2. _____

3. _____

4. _____

5. _____

Some habits, like anger, are driven by emotion. Some habits make up who you are. Although habits are voluntary, habits of fear, worry, and anxiety may feel involuntary. Habits will continue to feel involuntary until they are identified and confronted. Examples of bad habits you possess might include:

- *Yelling*
- *Worrying*
- *Smoking*
- *Lying*

My list of bad habits:

1. _____

2. _____

3. _____

4. _____

5. _____

Examples of good habits include the following

- *Journal writing*
- *Waking early*
- *Eating healthy*
- *Walking daily*

My list of good habits:

1. _____

2. _____

3. _____

4. _____

5. _____

REPLACEMENT EXERCISE

Write down a few of your bad habits in the table below then finish filling in the table with your chosen replacement habit you are going to try.

BAD HABIT	REPLACEMENT HABIT
Example: yelling	*Sing until the anger dissipates*

Notes

_____

_____

_____

_____

_____

Habits I learned from my parents:

1. _____

2. _____

3. _____

4. _____

5. _____

Now think of habits you continue from childhood and new habits you passed on to your children. Do the following exercise to bring those habits to a conscious level.

Habits I passed on to my children:

1. _____

2. _____

3. _____

4. _____

5. _____

EVALUATE YOUR HABITS

"Repetition is the mother of skill" rings true for good and bad habits. What shapes your life is not what you do once in a while but what you do consistently. Fill out the table below identifying what drives your actions and habits.

ACTION DRIVERS

I consistently	. . . precedes my action	. . . determines which action I take	. . . . drives my action
Example: eat sweets	*Stress*	*Degree of stress*	*emotion*
1.			
2.			
3.			
4.			
5.			

51

Notes

STEP FOUR: BE YOUR OWN CHANGE AGENT

Taking action is the element that transforms your dreams into reality. Where does the desire or power to initiate change come from? All of the resources needed to change and make your dreams a reality are within, lying dormant, storing energy for the day you transform your dreams into reality.

First, you have to wake up before you can claim your birthright. The power has always been within, ready to emerge at the time of breakthrough. Just like change, the breakthrough process does not happen in an instant and is not over in a moment.

Yes, sometimes change is immediate, and you receive instant feedback. This immediate or temporary change is what causes people to fail, leaving them disappointed. The unconscious fear of immediate or temporary change causes people to avoid lasting change. For example, you may lose weight on fad diets over several months until you meet your goal. As soon as you resume our old eating habits, you regain the weight plus some. The key to change is forming healthy, long-lasting habits.

You may not always be able to change your situation or circumstances, but you have the power to change your habits. The following exercises will help you change your habits.

A breakthrough results in irreversible change. Using the old standby example of dieting: What causes someone to put off dieting? Is it the unconscious fear of attempting something believed to be temporary? Will the sacrifice you have to endure in order to make the change bring a temporary reward? The following are three basic principles required for lasting change:

1. Change your expectations to a higher level; expect more of yourself.

Write down all the things to eliminate from your life, what you no longer will accept;
Example: I will no longer accept <u>negative people in my life</u>.

I will no longer accept_____

I will no longer accept_____

I will no longer accept _____

I will no longer accept_____

2. Change self-limiting beliefs (see replacement activities in STEP TWO: What is Not Working)

Write down the replacements you will make.
Example: I will replace worrying with positive affirmations.

I will replace _____ with _____.

I will replace _____ with _____.

I will replace _____ with _____.

I will replace _____ with _____.

3. Change your action plan; model your life after people who not only know what to do but actually do what they know. Studying successful people reminds you of what you already know, and then inspires you to do it.

Write the names of people you admire using the list from STEP ONE: Discover Your Purpose page 9.

_____   _____

_____   _____

_____   _____

_____   _____

IDENTIFY WHAT YOU MUST STOP BEFORE STARTING

The habit evaluation exercise should start you thinking about habits that impede your progress. In order to be prepared for the START, STOP, and CONTINUE exercise, think of habits you must STOP so you can START. The following list of bad habits provides some ideas on habits you should stop.

List of bad habits to STOP:

1. Punishing myself for past mistakes

2. Self-limiting thoughts (excuses)

3. Living someone else's expectations

4. Avoiding making life decisions

5. Distracting myself with task avoidance activities

6. Analysis paralysis-fear of failure and rejection

7. Procrastinating on the goals that matter

8. Personalizing the opinions of others

9. Choosing to do nothing

10. Focusing on the negative

EXAMPLE:

Desired result: By the end of the year I will finish my memoir

Behaviors to start:

1   *Write my annual goal and monthly benchmarks-revisit monthly to amend or revise.*

2   *Set my alarm at 5:00 a.m. daily.*

3   *Keep my work space organized and free of distractions.*

4   *Write 500 words per day in my memoir.*

5   *Write in my journal before retiring each day.*

Behaviors to stop:

1   *Sleeping in or hitting the snooze button.*

2   *Working in front of the TV.*

3   *Self-limiting beliefs about my ability to write.*

4   *Stop waiting for someone else to motivate me.*

5   *Waiting for just the right time to begin.*

Behaviors to continue:

1   *Listing my goals.*

2   *Organizing my photographs.*

3   *Talking to family members about my life.*

4   *Continue dreaming.*

5   *Reading other people's memoirs.*

Now it is your turn.

START, STOP, AND CONTINUE LIST

Desired result:

Behaviors to start:

1

2

3

4

5

Behaviors to stop:

1

2

3

4

5

Behaviors to continue:

1

2

3

4

5

EXERCISE: PARADIGM SHIFT

The following are some questions to ask when problem solving:

The problem:
Example: The problem is getting fired from my job.

What good can I find in this problem?
Example: This is a good opportunity to do something different.

What needs to be changed?
Example: My career choice needs to be changed.

What am I committed to do to make the change?
Example: I am committed to go to technical school.

What am I committed to stop doing in order to change?
Example: I am committed to stop blaming myself for getting fired.

How can I find joy in the journey toward change?
Example: I can find joy in learning something I am passionate about.

WHAT DO YOU DO WITH YOUR TIME?

People become what they value most. One of the prerequisites to change is having a sense of self.

Check your sense of self by asking the following questions:

What do I value most?
Example: relationships

Who do I honor most?
Example: spouse

What experiences are manifestations of who I am?
Example: Serving others

How you spend your days is how you spend your life.

1. **Choose two days (one a week day and one a weekend) to log your daily activities.**
   a. Charting or graphing creates a great visual picture of how you spend your time.
2. **Categorize by discretionary time and nondiscretionary time.**
   a. Activities categorized as discretionary can include watching TV, shopping, reading, exercising, etc.
   b. Activities categorized as nondiscretionary time includes sleeping, eating, working-essential life activities.

Use the calendar on the next page to log your activities.

MONDAY	**Discretionary:** **Nondiscretionary:**
TUESDAY	**Discretionary:** **Nondiscretionary:**
WEDNESDAY	**Discretionary:** **Nondiscretionary:**
THURSDAY	**Discretionary:** **Nondiscretionary:**
FRIDAY	**Discretionary:** **Nondiscretionary:**
SATURDAY	**Discretionary:** **Nondiscretionary:**
SUNDAY	**Discretionary:** **Nondiscretionary:**

One way to evaluate your sense of self is to assess how you focus your time and energy. Identifying activities during discretionary time reveals your priorities.

Assess your observation using the following questions:

What awaits me on the weekend?

Is it an activity totally different from what I do during the week that brings me joy?

Do I thrive during the work week and dread the weekend?

What part of the work week brings joy to my life?

Could those elements be extended into the weekend?

Do I have different priorities during the week day than on the weekend?

How do I spend my days off?

What do I do when I am bored?

What do I do out of habit (either good or bad)?

What part of my routine or habits would I never change?

What daily habits are unnecessary and do not contribute to my goals?

Which of the two days I tracked was the most enjoyable?

Notes

STEP FIVE: A CALL TO ACTION

What goals should you set? Set goals that require activities that help make you feel alive and fulfilled. Think of all the activities that make you the happiest and motivate you to take action. Make a list of all the activities you love to do because they make you happy.

My list of activities that I love to do because they make me happy:

Example: Writing in my journal

1. _____

2. _____

3. _____

4. _____

5. _____

As you brainstorm activities you love to do, observe the feelings, emotions, and passions. When specific activities create warm feelings and enthusiasm, you have identified the direction and focus of your goals. Go beyond the traditional New Year's resolutions and transcend from goal-setting to goal-getting.

Any feelings, emotions, passions I experienced when brainstorming:

Goal-getting requires a concerted effort to follow-up and follow-through on the small steps. Every day, calendars are filled with small tasks required for you to complete bigger goals. The following explains how to schedule priorities on your calendar. Just because the activity is on the schedule does not mean the task is a priority in fulfilling an intended goal. **Check the activities on your calendar to make sure they are aligned with your goals.**

List your goals

-
-
-
-

-
-
-
-

Calendar activities

-
-
-
-

-
-
-
-

Prioritize only those activities on your calendar that rank high on the tasks required for you to meet your goals. There will be certain tasks you may not want to do but are necessary for you to achieve your goals. Do not prioritize or set goals for accomplishing tasks you do not need or want to be doing at all. Experiment by placing unnecessary tasks at the bottom of the to-do list and see if they eventually fall off the list.

List activities on your calendar that are required for you to meet your goals. Rate each calendar activity using a scale of 1-10 with 1 being the lowest and 10 being the highest.

Calendar Activity	Scale (1-10)

Prioritize the calendar activities you rated according to scale rating. For example, number one below would be the highest ranking calendar activity, etc.:

1. _____

2. _____

3. _____

4. _____

5. _____

6. _____

7. _____

8. _____

9. _____

10. _____

The tasks with highest priority will go on week 1 and the not so important tasks on week 2. Eventually, the not so important tasks may fall off your to do list completely.

TO DO LIST

Week 1	Week 2
1.	6.
2.	7.
3.	8.
4.	9.
5.	10.

When you break down your project into smaller chunks, keep in mind the following three questions:

- What is the first thing I need to do?

- What comes after the first thing?

- What is the final step?

Calendar Activity Notes

_____

_____

_____

_____

_____

_____

_____

_____

_____

_____

_____

BENCHMARK ACTIVITY

Choose one goal for the following benchmark guided practice activity and write it down in the table on the next page.

Example: Long-term Goal--One year from today I will finish writing my memoir.

In the table write the benchmarks for achieving this goal. (You do not have to stick to the predefined benchmark periods)

Example:
Benchmark 1-One month from today I will complete the outline.

Benchmark 2-Six months from today I will send the draft manuscript to my editor.

Benchmark 3-One year from today I will publish my memoir on CreateSpace.

Create a data collection schedule that is realistic and attainable. Specific action steps will make monitoring progress easier. All action steps (goal-getting) must lead directly to the goal. Document the benchmark dates in your calendar to monitor your progress. Make sure the action steps are measurable. As you reach each benchmark evaluate your progress and alter the course or make modifications to your approach as needed. Flexibility based on information will help you make calculated decisions and help you recalculate as you navigate into uncharted territories.

Write down the four most important realistic tasks for each benchmark in the table. Work backwards from the outcome.

Goal (*Example: Start my own retail business*):
Year 5 Benchmark (*Example: apply for business loan***):**
Task 1
Task 2
Task 3
Task 4

Year 4 Benchmark *(Example: graduate)*:
Task 1
Task 2
Task 3
Task 4
Year 3 Benchmark *(Example: complete internship)***:**
Task 1
Task 2
Task 3
Task 4
Year 2 Benchmark *(Example: apply for internship)***:**
Task 1
Task 2
Task 3
Task 4

Year 1 Benchmark (*Example: maintain good grades*)**:**	
Task 1	
Task 2	
Task 3	
Task 4	
6 Month Benchmark (*Example: enroll in business college*)**:**	
Task 1	
Task 2	
Task 3	
Task 4	

Action Steps

In summary, laying the groundwork for fulfilling long-range goals comes down to the following five action steps:

1. Write down a single vision, project, or mission.

My goal that I choose to work on this year that is aligned with my purpose statement:

2. Set time aside to work on it every day.

The daily time I set aside to work on my goal:

3. Work consists of doing research, making connections, learning from projects similar to yours, challenging your assumptions, and seeking a mentor, partner, or confidant to bounce your ideas off of.

The person I will ask to be my mentor: _____

4. Set interim deadlines that you can reasonably meet every month.

   My interim deadlines:

   Month 1_____

   Month 2_____

   Month 3_____

   Month 4_____

   Month 5_____

5. **Be adaptable about changing your project as it unfolds.**

What activities are negotiable and will achieve the same result?

Negotiable:

What activities are nonnegotiable in your goal?

Nonnegotiable:

Do not wait for just the right time in your life to begin living intentionally. Instead of waiting for the time to be "just right," pick a date on your calendar and start from that day forth. If you start where you stand, you will attract the needed resources and tools to continue your quest for change.

Notes

_____

_____

_____

_____

Notes

STEP SIX: ASSESS YOUR PROGRESS

Record your goals and accomplishments along your journey; that way you can look back and measure your progress and recognize your transformation and breakthrough. The activities in Step Five: A Call to Action contain the information for your baseline that you will use to assess your progress. Success worth living is worth recording.

Practice the following steps when you evaluate your goals and benchmarks:

- At each milestone you achieve, amp up the expectations for the next benchmark in the goal-setting process.
- Self-monitor along the way, especially at each benchmark, by examining the information collected.
- Assess whether or not the benchmarks are set too high or too low. You will have to adjust accordingly.

In case you get stuck between working in small increments and forging ahead on your projects, here are a few suggestions to help you figure out what works best for you to push through the powerful force of resistance:

1. Perform the tiniest task you are willing to do.
2. If performing the tiniest task does not motivate you, then declare your refusal to do anything, at least until you are willing and able to do something.
3. Choose to complete a small part of a task that you are passionate about.
4. Program a reminder to complete a small task that includes something you love.
5. Record the task once completed and make plans to move toward the next incremental goal.

The conversation you have with yourself should narrow the discussion down to three simple questions:

- What is my purpose?
- What should I be doing?
- What is really worth doing?

Part of the evaluation process is to examine your actions and record your observations. Collect the data and record exactly what you find, not what you hope to find. For instance, record the number of benchmarks you achieved on schedule.

EVALUATION NOTES

EVALUATION NOTES

VISION/DREAM BOARD:

A vision or dream board is a powerful way to display your goals using images rather than words. Images evoke feelings and emotions compelling you to act on your goals. Visualize what your life will look like once you have achieved your goals.

Follow these simple steps to create your vision board:

1. You will need poster board, glue or tape, and scissors.
2. Collect a variety of magazines so you will have a broad range of images to depict your desired emotions that will motivate you to take action.
3. Place a picture of yourself in the center of the collage. Choose a picture that captures the ecstatic emotions of achieving your dreams. Organize the pictures in step 4 around the center picture of yourself.
4. Cut out images that convey messages of happiness. You can cut out words and sentences to create a visual of your dream goal. If your goal is to start your own business, then cut out a picture of a business front and cut and paste the words that you will name your business. Cut out images that will portray some of the benchmarks you will have to achieve on your way to goal. For instance, cut out a picture of a college graduation. Then cut out all the fun things you can do once you have a successful business. If you do not find the pictures you are looking for in magazines, then you can search on the Internet. The pictures you place on the poster board must motivate and inspire you.
5. Display your vision board in a place you will see daily. Invest five minutes every morning and evening looking at your board. Feel the emotions experienced from looking at what your life will look like when you have achieved your dreams.
6. Enjoy the journey!

You can search the Internet to look at numerous examples of vision (dream) boards.

Identifying measurable results as a requirement before taking action may not always be possible. The more you do what you are passionate about and love, the clearer the goals will become. The clearer the goals, the more concrete they will be, thus you will be more able to measure the results. Although results can be measured in different ways, time and resources are not always available. Different goals may require different methods of measurement. Do not let the measurement process stunt the imagination and creativity process of achieving your goals.

VISION/DREAM BOARD NOTES

(Ideas for your dream board, etc.)

_____

_____

_____

_____

_____

_____

_____

_____

_____

_____

_____

_____

_____

MEASURE YOUR GOALS

One way to measure non-quantifiable goals is to document the number of hours per week spent on achieving the goal. For instance, a goal aimed at improving your relationship with your spouse can be measured by the amount of time per day spent with your spouse.

Another way to measure non-quantifiable goals is to rate your "feeling" as you assess your goal. For example, at the end of each day rank your feeling of satisfaction toward your goal with 5 being "satisfactory" and 1 being "unsatisfactory." You can take this ranking system a step further and define "satisfactory" as "I did a kind deed for my spouse" and "unsatisfactory" as "I was not very kind to my spouse."

However you chose to measure your goals, it needs to be a realistic measurement and something that you personally translate as a measure of progress.

Be flexible with your measuring strategy. As you assess and refine your goals, the measurement system can be refined as you progress towards your goal outcome and as you become more aware of the measurable benefits. Do not just change the measurement system for the sake of showing progress if there really has not been any!

Managing progress is like launching a rocket-if your trajectory is off by inches at launch, you can be off by miles out in orbit. In other words, when moving quickly, it is important to make sure you have a firm foundation in place and a clear sense of your ultimate objective. Subsequently, the more specific you can be about who you are, the greater likelihood for success. You may either move so quickly you do not take time to define yourself or you define yourself too loosely (vision, mission, values blurred). You may get away with managing over the short term, mostly due to the momentum generated by your initial breakthrough. Take the trouble to talk the talk and walk the walk.

MEASUREMENTS/NOTES

DISCOVER YOUR PURPOSE, AGAIN

In Step One: Discover Your Purpose, you were asked to answer the questions below.
Now that you have completed the workbook, answer the following questions without looking back to your previous answers.

If I received what I asked for, what would I receive?

Am I ready for it right now?

If I had complete certainly I would succeed, what actions would I take to pursue my dreams?

What obstacles prevent me from achieving my dreams right now?

My Purpose Statement:

When you are finished answering the questions, go back to Step One: Discover Your Purpose and compare your answers. Did your answers change?

Do you need to revise your purpose statement?

Part of assessing your progress is to be sure your goals are still aligned with what you desire most in life. This passion for purpose will provide you with the capacity to persist all the way through to your transformation and breakthrough.

Goal setting is a fluid and dynamic process. Your priorities and therefore your goals will change as you grow older; which is why you should review and evaluate the goal setting process periodically to make sure your goals are still relevant to you. You are now equipped with the necessary skills and tools for life-no matter what stage of life you are in or your age.

Scheduling periodic reviews of your benchmarks and goals will give you early indications that your life may be taking a different route than originally planned. This is normal and expected as your life progresses. Changing your plans does not mean you have failed, it is just a way of refocusing your energy. Your benchmarks or short-term goals should also be flexible enough to accommodate changes in life such as getting married, having a child, or changing careers.

As you assess your goals you may discover they are not going exactly according to your action plan. This is okay as long as you are making progress in the right direction and you update your action plan so that it is still relevant and meaningful to you for achieving your goal.

NOTES

CONCLUSION

I hope you have learned a great deal of insight about yourself by completing the exercises in this workbook. Goal-setting to goal-getting is a personal journey, so it is important for you to know your strengths and what motivates you to take action. The personal questions are designed to help you understand yourself and ensure you are on the right journey.

Throughout ancient and modern history, many people have accomplished great achievements. The common denominator among successful people is that they set goals with a clear direction towards their chosen destination.

Setting goals is like a map—people who know where they are going and how to get there are more likely to get there than people who do not use a map. Goals show your target destination, and the benchmarks show the path or route to take on your map.

Hopefully, you are excited to find out how goal-setting works and how goal-getting can help you achieve your dreams. This workbook is intended to arm you with all the needed guidance to set your own personal goals and achieve success.

Goal setting is a life-long journey. Your goals will change along the way so evaluate often and make the necessary adjustments. As you become more experienced in the goal-setting and goal-getting process, you will feel a lot more confident in taking on multiple and more complex goals. Build on your experiences both good and bad and be the best that you can be and succeed!

www.ingramcontent.com/pod-product-compliance
Lightning Source LLC
Chambersburg PA
CBHW080524030426
42337CB00023B/4625